Contents

About *ISSUES* today

ISSUES today is a series of resource books on contemporary social issues, designed for Key Stage 3 pupils and above. This series is also suitable for Scottish P7, S1 and S2 students.

Each volume contains information from a variety of sources, including government reports and statistics, newspaper and magazine articles, surveys and polls, academic research and literature from charities and lobby groups. The information has been tailored to an 11 to 14 age group; it has been rewritten and presented in a simple, straightforward and accessible format.

In addition, each **ISSUES** today title features handy tasks and assignments based on the information contained in the book, for use in class, for homework or as a revision aid.

ISSUES today can be used as a learning resource in a variety of Key Stage 3 subjects, including English, Science, History, Geography, PSHE, Citizenship, Sex and Relationships Education and Religious Education.

About this book

Energy Choices is Volume 100 in the **ISSUES** today series.

Our non-renewable energy sources are running out; could we be possibly facing an energy crisis? It is time we considered future alternatives. This book looks at sustainable and renewable energy sources, as well as considering the most topical issues and debates such as smart meters, fracking and even 'poo power'.

Energy Choices offers a useful overview of the many issues involved in this topic. However, at the end of each article is a URL for the relevant organisation's website, which can be visited by pupils who want to carry out further research.

Because the information in this book is gathered from a number of different sources, pupils should think about the origin of the text and critically evaluate the information that is presented. Does the source have a particular bias or agenda? Are you being presented with facts or opinions? Do you agree with the writer?

At the end of each chapter there are two pages of activities relating to the articles and issues raised in that chapter. The 'Brainstorm' questions can be done as a group or individually after reading the articles. This should prompt some ideas and lead on to further activities. Some suggestions for such activities are given under the headings 'Oral', 'Moral dilemmas', 'Research', 'Written' and 'Design' that follow the 'Brainstorm' questions.

For more information about **ISSUES** today and its sister series, **ISSUES** (for pupils aged 14 to 18), please visit the Independence website.

Renewable energy vs non-renewable energy

By Kelly Fenn

The chief contributor to climate change is carbon emissions from fossil fuels. However, with those finite fuel sources running out, considering new forms of energy won't just be good for the environment, it will be absolutely important in years to come. For now, a commitment to renewable energy is on the world political agenda, with Europe, for example, proposing a target of increasing total use of renewable energy from 7% to 20% by 2020.

Take a look into how each source of energy, renewable and non-renewable, compare.

Coal

Coal has the most widely distributed reserves in the world and is mined in over 100 countries. While scientists believe there are still enough reserves of coal to serve the world's energy needs for some years to come, the impact of burning coal is environmentally devastating.

Burning coal is a leading cause of smog, acid rain and toxic substances in the air, and one of the chief culprits of carbon dioxide emissions. In an average year, a typical coal power station generates 3,700,000 tons of carbon dioxide, and is the main human cause of global warming – that's as much carbon dioxide as cutting down 161 million trees.

Oil

Oil and petroleum products supply a third of the primary energy used in the UK. One of the chief problems with reliance on oil is the difficulty and cost involved in drilling for and gathering it – meaning the cost of wholesale oil is continuing to rise. Oil spillages during transportation also pose serious risks to the environment and wildlife. Additionally, burning oil also has a grave environmental impact.

Oil is the most commonly reported cause of water pollution, with over 5,000 incidents recorded annually by the Environment Agency. A single litre of oil spilled can contaminate a million litres of drinking water. And overall, 30% of CO_2 emissions affecting the atmosphere come from cars and other petrol-guzzling vehicles.

Gas

Natural gas burns cleaner that the other fossil fuels and produces less greenhouse gases when processed. For an equivalent amount of heat, burning natural gas produces about 30% less carbon dioxide than burning petroleum and about 45% less than burning coal.

Before natural gas can be used as a fuel, it undergoes extensive processing to remove other materials contained in the gas, meaning that other gases escape into the air. Crucially, scientists suggest that reserves of gas will run out by 2085.

Nuclear

Nuclear energy is energy released from the atomic nucleus. Nuclear is a clean form of energy in that it releases almost none of the CO_2 emissions associated with fossil fuels.

While the amount of energy that can be produced through nuclear power is significant, so too are the possible side effects. Disposing of radioactive nuclear waste is a serious issue to consider. Nuclear energy is a controversial source of energy, with the effects caused by nuclear spills such as the Chernobyl disaster having long-term and negative effects on the environment and human health.

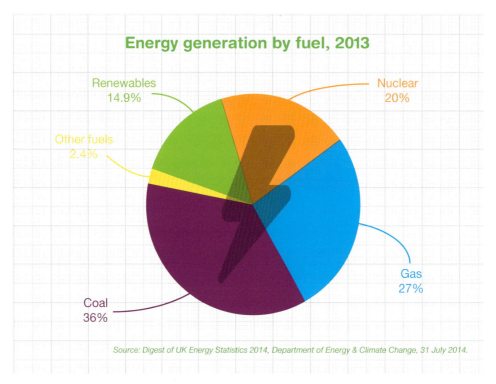

Energy generation by fuel, 2013

- Renewables 14.9%
- Nuclear 20%
- Other fuels 2.4%
- Gas 27%
- Coal 36%

Source: Digest of UK Energy Statistics 2014, Department of Energy & Climate Change, 31 July 2014.

Wind

Wind farms are one of the fastest growing green sources of electricity generation. With the UK possessing 40% of Europe's total wind resource, wind power offers a tempting alternative to fossil fuel power, and it's also renewable and emission free.

In the future, if wind energy were to provide a significantly larger chunk of global energy, then the land needed for wind farms would have a big impact on more and more people's living space. There are also concerns that wind farms offshore interrupt ecosystems and local wildlife. Another complaint is that wind farms are ugly and noisy.

Hydro

Tidal and river water flow can be harnessed to create energy, and with the UK being surrounded by water, appears to be a logical energy option. River hydro stations aren't considered to be a serious option due to the ecological impact on the local environment. However, tidal hydro-power stations are growing in technological capabilities, with research and trials continuing. It's not yet as developed as other renewable technologies but certainly one to watch.

Solar

Transforming naturally occurring light rays into energy is a logical and sustainable source of energy. In spite of the short summers and cloudy skies, the UK still receives 50% of the sunlight per square foot as countries on the equator. Solar energy is popular and working well in other European countries, and could serve the UK similarly.

However, there are limitations to the technology that will need improvement so the process is optimised and more efficient – for example, the photovoltaic cells used in the process of solar harnessing only currently absorb around 15% of the sunlight's energy.

1 July 2014

www.energysavingsecrets.co.uk

Mini glossary

Extensive – *quite a lot.*

Petroleum – *also called crude oil, this is a dark, thick oil obtained from under the ground. It is used to make a number of different things such as petrol, paraffin and diesel oil.*

Finite – *will eventually run out, will not last, will end.*

Digest of UK Energy Statistics 2014

The Department of Energy & Climate Change today releases four key publications: the *Digest of United Kingdom Energy Statistics 2014*, *UK Energy in Brief*, *Energy Flow Chart* and *Energy Consumption in the United Kingdom* providing detailed analysis of production, transformation and consumption of energy in 2013.

Key points

- Primary energy production fell by 6.3 per cent, on a year earlier, due to record low coal output following mine closures; oil and gas output were also down as output facilities were affected by maintenance issues alongside longer term decline.
- Final energy consumption rose by 0.7 per cent, reflecting the colder weather in 2013. On a temperature adjusted basis, energy consumption was down 0.3 per cent continuing the downward trend of the last nine years.
- Electricity generated from renewable sources in the UK in 2013 increased by 30 per cent on a year earlier, and accounted for 14.9 per cent of total UK electricity generation, up from 11.3 per cent in 2012. Total renewables, as measured by the 2009 EU Renewables Directive, accounted for 5.2 per cent of energy consumption in 2013, up from 4.2 per cent in 2012.
- In 2013, the UK became a net importer of petroleum products for the first time since 1984 (the year of the miner's strike) and before that 1973; largely due to the closure of the Coryton Refinery in July 2012.

Main energy production and trade statistics:

- Primary energy production fell by 6.3 per cent in 2013, following the record falls of 13.4 and 10.8 per cent in the previous two years. Production has now fallen in each year since 1999, and is now less than half its 1999 levels, an average annual rate of decline of 6.6 per cent.
- Gross natural gas production fell 6.2 per cent in 2013. This reflects the continuing long-term decline in UK natural gas production, which has fallen by an average of 8.0 per cent per year since 2000, when production peaked.
- Crude oil (including NGLs) production in 2013 was 8.8 per cent lower than in 2012 at 41 million tonnes. Production has fallen by 70 per cent from its 1999 peak.

- Coal production was down by 25 per cent in 2013 compared to 2012, following the closure of a number of mines.
- Energy imports were at record levels in 2013, up 2.3 per cent on 2012 levels
  - For crude oil, the key source was Norway which accounted for 40 per cent of imports, with a large growth in imports from Algeria and Saudi Arabia.
  - For gas the key source was also Norway, which accounted for 58 per cent of UK imports, with 16 per cent from The Netherlands. LNG accounted for 20 per cent of gas imports, down from 28 per cent in 2012, with 93 per cent of these imports from Qatar.
  - The UK sources its petroleum products widely, with a range of European countries supplying diesel road fuel. Aviation fuel is also sourced widely with significant volumes from OPEC countries such as Kuwait and Saudi Arabia. The UK, though, remains a net exporter of petrol with 35 per cent of exports shipped to the USA.
  - For coal the key source was Russia, accounting for 41 per cent of UK imports, followed by the USA and Colombia which accounted for 25 and 23 per cent, respectively.
- The UK remained a net importer of energy, with an increased dependency level (imports/energy use) of 47 per cent; this continues the trend from 2004 when the UK once again became a net importer of fuel. In 2013 the UK was a net importer of all fuels, as imports of petroleum products in total exceeded exports following the closure of the Coryton refinery.

Main energy consumption statistics:

- UK primary energy consumption in 2013 decreased by 0.6 per cent, and on a temperature-adjusted basis, consumption was down 1.9 per cent, continuing the downward trend of the last eight years.

- Overall gas demand decreased by 1.1 per cent. Gas demand for electricity generation decreased by 5.7 per cent as gas's share of the UK's generation of electricity fell to 27 per cent, from 28 per cent last year. Domestic demand was similar to that in 2012.
- Total oil consumption in the UK saw a small fall down by one per cent when compared with 2012. Over 70 per cent of oil is consumed in the transport sector, which showed little change in overall consumption from 2012.
- Consumption of diesel road fuel exceeded the consumption of motor spirit in 2013 by over nine million tonnes. Up until 2005, motor spirit exceeded diesel road fuel sales, since then a large element of the UK's car fleet has switched to diesel. Petrol consumption has fallen by around four per cent per annum in the past ten years, whilst diesel use has increased by nearly two per cent per annum, over the same period.
- Coal consumption decreased by 5.7 per cent in 2013. There was a 7.4 per cent decrease in consumption by major power producers (consumers of 83 per cent of total coal demand) reflecting lower demand and more renewables. Coal accounted for 36 per cent of the electricity generated in the UK in 2013, down from 39 per cent in 2012. The domestic sector accounted for only 1.1 per cent of total coal consumption.
- Energy consumption by final users at 142.5 million tonnes of oil equivalent increased by 0.7 per cent in 2013. Consumption in the domestic sector was broadly unchanged, up only 0.2 per cent; with industry and service sector use up by 2.4 and 3.1 per cent, respectively. There was reduced consumption from transport, which was down 0.7 per cent. Average temperatures in 2013 were marginally cooler than in 2012. On a temperature-adjusted basis final energy consumption was down by 0.3 per cent continuing the downward trend of the last nine years.
- Refinery production decreased by six per cent on 2012 and 25 per cent on 2000. The closure of the Coryton refinery contributed to the decrease in production as it had been operating in the first half of 2012. Production was dented further by the temporary closure of the Grangemouth refinery in October 2013. Imports of petroleum product imports have increased by eight per cent to make up the shortfall. In addition, exports have decreased by three per cent, as a result the UK was a net importer of petroleum products in 2013 for the first time since 1984, the year of the miners' strike. Petrol accounts for over a third of exports.

Main electricity generation and supply statistics:

Gas prices remained high in 2013, such that the commercial attractiveness of gas for electricity generation continued to be weak in 2013. Meanwhile, nuclear's share of electricity generation was unchanged, despite a slight increase in generation. Gas accounted for 27 per cent of electricity supplied in 2013, with coal accounting for 36 per cent and nuclear 20 per cent.

- Electricity generated from renewable sources in the UK in 2013 increased by 30 per cent on a year earlier, and accounted for 14.9 per cent of total UK electricity generation, up from 11.3 per cent in 2012. Offshore wind generation increased by 50 per cent, and onshore wind increased by 40 per cent. Both the offshore and onshore wind load factors (37.5 per cent and 27.9 per cent) exceeded or equalled that of gas (27.9 per cent).
- In 2013, the proportion of UK electricity generated from renewables was 14.9 per cent. Installed electrical generating capacity of renewable sources rose by 27 per cent (4.2 GW) in 2013, mainly as a result of a 27 per cent increase (1.6 GW) in onshore wind capacity, 59 per cent increase (1.0 GW) in solar photovoltaic capacity (due to high deployment of both small-scale capacity under Feed in Tariffs and large-scale capacity under the Renewables Obligation). Bioenergy capacity increased by 27 per cent (0.8 GW) due to new conversions of previously coal-fired capacity to biomass.
- There was a 0.5 per cent decrease in the total supply of electricity in the UK in 2013, to 373.6 TWh. Indigenous electricity supply fell by one per cent, but net imports of electricity increased by around 20 per cent, to 14.5 TWh, as imports rose substantially more than exports.
- Final consumption of electricity was broadly unchanged at 317.3 TWh, the lowest level since 1998.
- The domestic sector was the largest electricity consumer in 2013 (113.5 TWh), while the industrial sector consumed 98.0 TWh and the service sector consumed 101.7 TWh. Industrial consumption increased by 0.2 per cent, while domestic consumption fell by 1.1 per cent.

Other energy statistics:

- Total renewables, as measured by the 2009 EU Renewables Directive, accounted for 5.2 per cent of energy consumption in 2013 up from 4.2 per cent in 2012.

➤ In 2013, Combined Heat and Power (CHP) capacity stood at 6,170 MWe, a small decrease on 2012.

➤ In 2013 the energy industries accounted for 3.3 per cent of GDP.

The fuel switching away from gas and coal for electricity generation, with other changes, is provisionally estimated to have decreased emissions of carbon dioxide by around two per cent in 2013.

Energy consumption in the United Kingdom

➤ Final energy consumption, excluding non-energy use, rose by 0.9 million tonnes of oil equivalent (mtoe) from 141.5 to 142.5 mtoe between 2012 and 2013 – an increase of one per cent.

➤ Energy consumption in 2013 was 16.9 mtoe lower than in 2000 (142.5 mtoe compared to 159.4 mtoe) – a decrease of 11 per cent, and two per cent lower than in 1970.

➤ In 2013, energy consumption in the industrial sector increased by two per cent since 2012, with the iron and steel sector showing a 17 per cent increase to 1.3 mtoe. The largest energy consuming single sub-sector in the industrial sector was chemicals, which accounted for 14 per cent of all industrial energy consumption. Energy consumption per unit of output fell by 53 per cent in the chemicals sector between 2000 and 2013, while there was a fall of eight per cent in the same measure for the iron and steel sector; for all industries there was a fall of 19 per cent.

➤ Energy consumption in the transport sector decreased by 0.7 per cent between 2012 and 2013. Transport energy consumption fell four per cent (2.0 mtoe) between 2000 and 2013, with the largest actual decrease occurring in the road transport sector, where consumption fell by four per cent (18 mtoe) – with this sector accounting for 74 per cent of total transport consumption in 2013. Over the same period, air transport fuel increased by two per cent since 2000 and rail transport use fell by 23 per cent.

➤ In 2013, domestic energy consumption remained stable with consumption in 2012 (0.2 per cent increase) – similar levels of consumption to 2009. The intermediate years had unusual weather spells (the high levels of consumption in 2010 were largely driven by colder temperatures and the lower levels of consumption in 2011 were due to a warmer than usual heating season).

➤ The seven per cent decrease in consumption since 2000 is set in the context of an increase of 11 per cent in the number of UK households and a nine per cent increase in the UK population. At a per household level, energy consumption has fallen by nine per cent since 2000.

➤ In the service sector, energy consumption n the private commercial sector increased by 30 per cent between 2000 and 2013, in the public sector it fell by 23 per cent and by 23 per cent in the agriculture sector. Over the same period, output, measured as the contribution made to the UK economy, increased by 35 per cent in the private sector and increased by 23 per cent in the public sector, in real terms.

31 July 2014

www.gov.uk

Mini Glossary

GW – Short for gigawatt, this is a large unit of measurement that represents the rate of energy transfer. A gigawatt is equal to one billion watts.

LNG – Liquefied Natural Gas. This is when a natural gas, such as methane, has been converted into liquid form so that is it easier to store and transport.

OPEC countries – Members of the Organization of the Petroleum Exporting Countries. This organisation monitors the supply, price and sale of petroleum, aiming to make sure that the price of petroleum does not change too much and to ensure a regular supply of petroleum oil to other countries. Algeria, Iran, Qatar and Venezuela are a few examples of OPEC countries.

NGLs – Natural Gas Liquids.

TW – Short for terawatt, this is a large unit of measurement that represents the rate of energy transfer. A terawatt is equal to one trillion watts. TWh refers to how many terawatts per hour.

Energy prices rise forcing changes in lifestyle

By Ben Tobin

A recent YouGov Reports publication has found that three in ten are spending 10% or more of their household income on gas and electricity, as the debate surrounding energy prices rages on in the Commons and beyond.

Of those in this group, many say they have had to make changes to their lives in order to pay the bills. Almost seven in ten (68%) say they have turned the heating down or off when they ordinarily would have left it on, 27% have spent less on food while 5% have borrowed from short term lenders in order to fulfil bills. 44% of those not in this group say they have had to reduce their usage.

Negative opinions towards energy suppliers and prices are commonplace. 84% agree that companies are quick to raise prices when their costs go up, but slower in offering discounts when they fall. Over two thirds (67%) agree that big energy suppliers act as a cartel, while 66% say the electricity and gas supply market has major problems which the Government needs to address. Half (50%) believe UK household energy bills are some of the highest in Europe. Only 9% say big suppliers treat their customers fairly.

Changes to the market

In terms of changes to the market, 69% favour forcing energy supplies to reduce the number of different tariffs they offer and simplify bills. Over half (52%) are positive towards the use of one-off windfall taxes on profits of large energy supplies to help cut household bills, or to support infrastructure needs. 51% support freezing household energy prices for 20 months from May 2015 and 46% would like to see greater regulation in order to force greater competition.

Tom Rees, UK Research Manager at YouGov Reports, said; 'Our research indicates how little consumers trust energy suppliers, the high level of dissatisfaction with the energy market and the tangible effect on household finances. Whether this will lead to consumers switching providers in greater numbers remains to be seen, and the question of what the Government should do will be crucial in the lead up to next May's election.'

19 June 2014

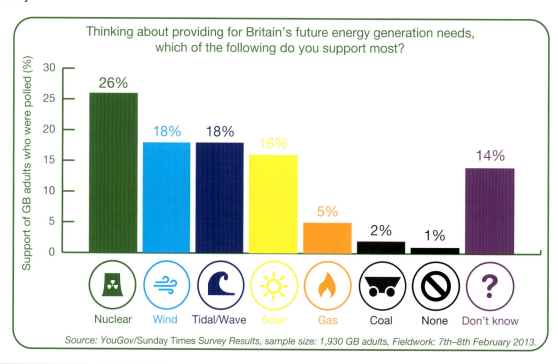

Thinking about providing for Britain's future energy generation needs, which of the following do you support most?

Support of GB adults who were polled (%)

Nuclear 26% · Wind 18% · Tidal/Wave 18% · Solar 16% · Gas 5% · Coal 2% · None 1% · Don't know 14%

Source: YouGov/Sunday Times Survey Results, sample size: 1,930 GB adults, Fieldwork: 7th–8th February 2013.

Mini glossary

Tariff *– a tariff is a fixed-price charge by a business.*

www.yougov.co.uk

Half of UK householders think it's cheaper to leave the home heating on all day at low temperature

Energy Saving Trust launches energy saving mythbusters in bid to help UK householders cut fuel bills.

Half (50 per cent) of all UK householders think it's cheaper to leave their home heating on all day than turning the heating on or off and up or down when required.

This finding is part of an energy saving mythbusting survey commissioned by the Energy Saving Trust as part of Big Energy Saving Week, which highlights the perceptions of the UK public and how they don't always match the reality of the energy saving action or statement.

The survey was carried out to a sample of 2,067 online adults in the UK aged 16–75 earlier this month.

Other findings from the Ipsos MORI survey include:

- ➤ 30 per cent that think screensavers on computers save energy.
- ➤ Almost half (45 per cent) think switched-off electrical appliances don't use electricity when they're plugged in at the mains.
- ➤ Nearly half (48 per cent) agreed that it's a hassle to change energy suppliers.
- ➤ Two thirds (66 per cent) of people think that more heat is lost through the roof of their home than the walls – however, for the majority of properties the walls will actually lose more heat.

However, there were other findings which highlighted a level of awareness from the UK public regarding the correct energy saving actions to take in the home. These include:

- ➤ Just 27 per cent incorrectly said turning up their thermostat to a high setting heats the home faster, compared to 54 per cent that correctly said the statement was false.
- ➤ Three quarters (75 per cent) know that energy saving light bulbs are compatible with traditional light bulb fittings.
- ➤ And, 69 per cent know that solar panels will work during daylight hours regardless of whether the sun is shining or not, with only ten per cent disagreeing.

Energy Saving Trust chief executive Phillip Sellwood said: 'We commissioned this survey to bust some of the top energy saving myths we encounter on a daily basis. While for certain actions a portion of the UK public think they are saving energy when they're not, it's heartening to see that a lot of people are doing the right thing in the home to save energy.

'We know it's important for the UK public to stay warm and cosy in their homes. But for the majority the most cost-effective way to do this is to turn the heating on and off or up and down when required rather than leaving it on all day at a lower temperature. This ensures that heat is not wasted and that your home will be at a comfortable temperature.

'Our message to UK householders is clear: if you don't know where to start when it comes to saving energy and cutting your fuel bill, or just need some advice, visit the Energy Saving Trust website or give the Energy Saving Advice Service a call on 0300 123 1234 for independent and impartial advice.

'Throughout Big Energy Saving Week, the Energy Saving Trust and partners will provide practical solutions and advice to help households save money on their energy bills. For us, saving energy – not wasting it – is the right thing to do and makes total sense.'

According to figures from the Energy Saving Trust, the UK could collectively save nearly £4.4 billion on energy bills if householders took three energy saving actions in the home.

These are:

➢ **Turn it off** – Make sure you turn your lights, appliances and chargers off when you're not using them. Virtually all electrical and electronic appliances can safely be turned off at the plug without upsetting their systems.

➢ **Turn it down** – Many households have their central heating set higher than they need, without even realising it. If it's too warm inside, try turning your room thermostat down by one degree and see if you are still at a comfortable temperature. Every degree that you turn it down will make additional savings to your heating bill.

➢ **Let there be light** – Households can now get LED spotlights that are bright enough to replace halogens, as well as regular energy saving bulbs ('compact fluorescent lamps' or CFLs) for pretty much everything else. They come in a variety of shapes, sizes and fittings and can save households money on their energy bills.

Big Energy Saving Week took place between Monday 27 and Friday 31 January, with the week aiming to raise awareness of energy and efficiency issues among the UK public through joint working between the voluntary sector and energy suppliers.

The week has taken place twice previously and is funded by the largest six energy companies, with involvement from Citizens Advice Bureau, Energy Saving Trust, Age UK, ACRE (Action with Communities in Rural England), Consumer Futures, the Department of Energy and Climate Change (DECC), Ofgem, Energy UK and National Energy Action.

To find out more visit www.bigenergysavingweek.org.uk or call 0300 123 1234.

Ten energy saving myths

1 Leaving the heating on all day on a low temperature is cheaper than turning the heating up and down or on and off as needed.

FALSE: For the majority of householders leaving your room thermostat on all day at a lower temperature will not only mean that your home will never be at a comfortable temperature but it will also waste heat when you do not need it. Room thermostats turn the heat on and off when your home reaches the set temperature that you feel comfortable at. Combine this with a timer control that tells your heating system to come on only when you need it to save money on your energy bills.

2 Cranking up the thermostat heats your home faster.

FALSE: Your room thermostat turns your heating system on or off according to a set temperature. No matter how high you set the temperature, the rate at which your central heating distributes heat remains constant. To heat your home faster, install better insulation. This decreases the rate at which heat is lost through your walls, loft, windows and floor – heating your home faster and keeping it warm for longer.

3 Electrical appliances, such as TVs, laptops, phone chargers, etc., don't use electricity when they're plugged-in but not in-use.

FALSE: Some electrical appliances and chargers draw energy even when the devices are not being used. This 'vampire power' wastes energy, and the best way to avoid this is to remember to switch off at the wall and pull out the plug.

By avoiding standby, and making sure devices are not left plugged in or idle, a typical home could save between £50-£80 a year.*

*Based all home appliances, consumer electronics, lights and chargers that have been left on standby mode or have been left on and not in use, using the average electricity cost of 13.52p/kWh. Sourced from DEFRA's Home Electricity Study.

4 It is cheaper to run appliances, such as washing machines, at night than during the day.

This may be true, but not for most of us. While some households in the UK are on tariffs that vary depending on the time of day, such as Economy 7, the majority of customers pay the same rate at all times of day and night. However, if you know you are already on an Economy tariff, or are considering switching to one, then running appliances during off-peak periods will be cheaper.

5 With traditional light-bulb fittings, you cannot do a straightforward swap with energy saving bulbs and LED light bulbs.

FALSE: Energy saving and LED light bulbs come in all shapes and sizes and can now be fitted in down-lighters, free-standing lamps and traditional pendants.

6 Putting plastic tape and a layer of cling-film around draughty windows is a better option at keeping heat in the home than draught excluders or double glazing.

FALSE: Although physically blocking gaps around your windows with cling film or plastic tape may stop draughts and reduce heat loss, this will not be as effective as draught excluders or double glazing. These more permanent measures reduce heat loss more effectively – keeping your home warmer and saving money on your heating bills.

7 Cavity wall insulation causes damp in the home.

FALSE: In most cases cavity wall insulation is likely to help reduce damp in the home, not make it worse. A combination of proper insulation, ventilation and balanced heating in a home will help avoid cold spots and moisture from condensing on your walls. Assessors should be able to advise you as to whether your home is suitable for insulation and any potential risk from damp.

8 Solar panels don't generate electricity on a cloudy day.

FALSE: Whilst solar panels will work most effectively in bright sunlight, they nonetheless continue to collect energy from diffuse light even on a cloudy day. Summer months are the most productive as there are longer daylight hours than in winter.

9 When using a desktop computer, screensavers save energy.

FALSE: Because your screen remains on, screensavers are basically another program which consumes energy like any other. While computers have timed sleep settings which do use less energy, switching off your monitor or even your whole computer when taking breaks is the most effective way to stop energy being wasted.

On average desktop computers cost around £24 a year to run.*

Based all home appliances, consumer electronics, lights and chargers that have been left on standby mode or have been left on and not in use, using the average electricity cost of 13.52p/kWh. Sourced from DEFRA's Home Electricity Study.

10 It's difficult and a hassle to switch energy suppliers.

FALSE: There are a number of energy price comparison companies where you can find the cheapest tariff for your area by checking online or by telephone. Once you have filled in the application with your main details, which typically takes around half an hour, the energy provider will sort the switch for you. Finding the deal that's best for you, and switching energy supplier, can be a great way to reduce your energy bills.

www.energysavingtrust.org.uk

Energy efficient buildings – beware possible health risks

An article from The Conversation.

THE CONVERSATION

By Melissa C. Lott – PhD Student: energy, environmental and public health trade-offs of energy system technology transitions, focusing on air pollution at University College London

The primary goal of home energy efficiency initiatives might be to reduce total energy consumption, but these projects could have a negative impact on public health if we do not take care.

Global climate change has been called the biggest global public health threat of the 21st century – and energy efficiency is a key tool in our efforts to reduce greenhouse gas emission levels.

Efficiency projects allow us to more effectively manage growing energy consumption without sacrificing services that we value. In the cost-optimised 2°C scenario set out by the International Energy Agency (the temperature rise that we have to stick within if we're to mitigate climate change), end-use efficiency improvements will be responsible for 38% of the global emissions reductions between now and 2050.

Without these emissions decreases, the World Health Organization expects 250,000 additional deaths to occur each year, caused by climate-related malnutrition, malaria, diarrhoea and heat stress around the globe.

Given these numbers, it seems logical to push forward with blanketing energy efficiency investments. However, there is evidence to show that we must take care in how we implement projects.

In a 2014 article published in the *British Medical Journal*, James Milner and his co-authors outlined how some home energy

efficiency improvements could cost lives by increasing indoor radon exposure and the risk of developing lung cancer.

According to the authors, energy efficiency projects could lead to an estimated 56.6% increase in average indoor radon concentrations. They calculate that the corresponding increase in radon exposure could lead to 278 premature deaths (the equivalent of 4,700 life years lost) each year in the UK.

After smoking, radon exposure is the most important risk factor in developing lung cancer. This colourless gas, which occurs naturally from the indirect decay product of uranium or thorium, can be found in indoor air. It produces a radioactive dust that is trapped in our airways. This radiation then causes lung damage and increases the chance that we will develop lung cancer. Each year, an estimated 1,400 cases of lung cancer in the UK are primarily due to radon exposure and about 21,000 in the US.

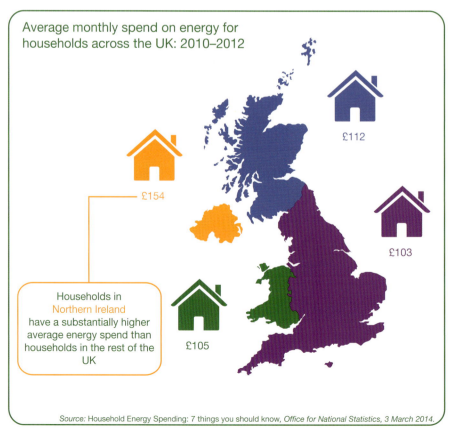

Average monthly spend on energy for households across the UK: 2010–2012

£154

£112

£103

£105

Households in Northern Ireland have a substantially higher average energy spend than households in the rest of the UK

Source: Household Energy Spending: 7 things you should know, *Office for National Statistics, 3 March 2014.*

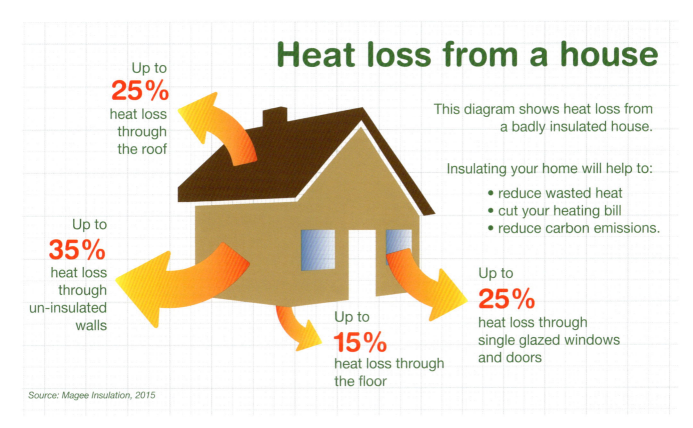

Heat loss from a house

Up to **25%** heat loss through the roof

This diagram shows heat loss from a badly insulated house.

Insulating your home will help to:
- reduce wasted heat
- cut your heating bill
- reduce carbon emissions.

Up to **35%** heat loss through un-insulated walls

Up to **15%** heat loss through the floor

Up to **25%** heat loss through single glazed windows and doors

Source: Magee Insulation, 2015

The increased radon concentrations in the Milner study stem from the fact that many energy efficiency improvements alter the way that buildings exchange indoor and outdoor air. These alterations are often aimed at reducing energy losses due to leaky windows or drafts around unsealed doors. In turn, these buildings can be more effectively heated and cooled, leading to observable public health improvements and decreases in total energy use.

However, they can increase some health risks. According to Milner and co-authors, while an individual project can be 'good for energy efficiency, indoor temperatures in winter and protection against outdoor pollutants, it has the potential to increase concentrations of pollutants arising from sources inside or underneath the home'.

A 2013 study suggested similar risks in retrofitted buildings from mould growth and 'sick building syndrome', where occupants appear to experience health issues from occupancy in a building. By trapping humidity inside the building, energy efficiency retrofits could unintentionally lead to dangerous mould growth. In turn, people in these buildings would be more prone to chronic fatigue, irritated lungs and watery eyes.

Using fans and other equipment to carefully control the indoor air quality could reduce or eliminate the negative co-impacts documented in these studies. Of course, the use of these technologies would offset some of the energy savings. But, they could also prevent an array of illnesses, which could stymie future energy efficiency proposals.

Energy efficiency projects can help to reduce total energy consumption. They are a key part of mitigating the impacts of global climate change. But we must be aware of any potential negative co-impacts on human health and take care to reduce their effect.

23 September 2014

www.theconversation.com

Mini glossary

Mitigate – *to lessen the impact of something, to make something less severe/painful.*

Stymie – *to prevent something.*

Activities

Brainstorm

1.   What is renewable energy?

2.   What is non-renewable energy?

Oral activity

3.   Discuss as a class what it means to be 'energy efficient'.

Research activities

4.   Devise and carry out a survey among your year group to assess their attitudes towards different types of energy. It should contain no more than ten questions and you should have at least 15 respondents. Do your results show much diversity in people's opinions?

5.   How much electricity do you use in a day? Keep an energy diary over the course of one day, recording every time you switch on a light, boil a kettle, watch television, etc. and how long before you turn each device off again. Are you surprised by how much you rely on electricity?

Written activity

6.   Read *Energy efficient buildings – beware possible health risks* (page 10) and write a short summary of this article.

Moral dilemma

7.   A recent YouGov Reports publication has found that three in ten are spending 10% or more of their household income on gas and electricity. How can we tackle this issue?

Design activities

8.   Design a poster which helps bust energy saving myths in a bid to help UK householders cut fuel bills. You might want to include commonly incorrect statements and correct them and/or tips on how to be energy efficient. You might find reading *Half of UK householders think it's cheaper to leave the home heating on all day at low temperature* (page 7) helpful.

9.   Design an informative leaflet which shows all the different types of energy available, listing the pros and cons of each.

Power to the people – smart meters, lower energy bills?

Even though the price of your next energy bills may shock you, will you spend any time at all doing something about it?

Faced with above-inflation hikes in energy costs, the government has advised customers to try switching to save money.

But a recent study by Accenture concluded that the average customer spends only nine minutes a year interacting with their energy provider, typically on matters relating to billing, credit or supply issues.

So if high prices don't prompt us to act, what will? Social scientists believe they know.

In a study in California in San Marcos ten years ago researchers found that the single most effective way to get people to change their energy use, was to tell them how much more their neighbours were doing to save energy.

So in the spirit of journalistic enquiry (and in some trepidation), I sent nine of my near neighbours – all in similar terraced houses – an e-mail revealing how much my family spends a month on gas and electricity.

Immediately a neighbour who also has teenage children e-mailed back, wanting to know how I got our bills so much lower than hers. Others replied with tales of how they were changing supplier or replacing their boilers.

Behavioural science

It's an impulse that the energy suppliers know all about.

On 1 October, Eon launched a new facility on their website allowing customers to check out the energy bills of similar properties nearby and 360,000 customers have already logged on to use it.

As well as graphicising monthly energy use compared to similar homes in their area, Eon's Saving Energy Toolkit also gives a 'what uses most' chart showing how energy is currently being used in a customer's home and tailored tips on how to reduce energy use.

British Gas run a similar scheme – they've even called it 'Keeping up with the neighbours'.

The data generated by Eon's Toolkit is based on old-fashioned meter readings or estimates. But soon those will be a thing of the past.

> *'The average customer spends only nine minutes a year interacting with their energy provider, typically on matters relating to billing, credit or supply issues.'*

By 2020, the Government wants all homes and small businesses to have smart meters fitted. That means replacing over 53 million gas and electricity meters in 30 million properties.

Smart meters will not only send gas and electricity readings back to suppliers automatically – making estimated bills history – but can also be attached to a display unit that lets customers see how much energy they are using on a minute-by-minute basis.

It's a natural progression Stuart Rolland, Managing Director of British Gas Smart Metering told Channel 4 News.

'Smart metering is bringing energy into the digital era, as banking and retail was nine to ten years ago. The customer gets the benefit of true insight, and with that control and the ability to save money,' he said.

Over 350,000 British Gas customers are already using smart meters and the company hopes to install a further half a million next year.

Customer engagement

Users get a monthly smart energy report online or on paper, detailing where energy is used and where their money goes.

Remember that Accenture statistic about our interaction with our suppliers? (Just nine minutes a year on average.)

British Gas says that 30 per cent of smart meter households spend an average of 18 minutes looking at their monthly energy reports – not once, but five times a year.

But that's not all.

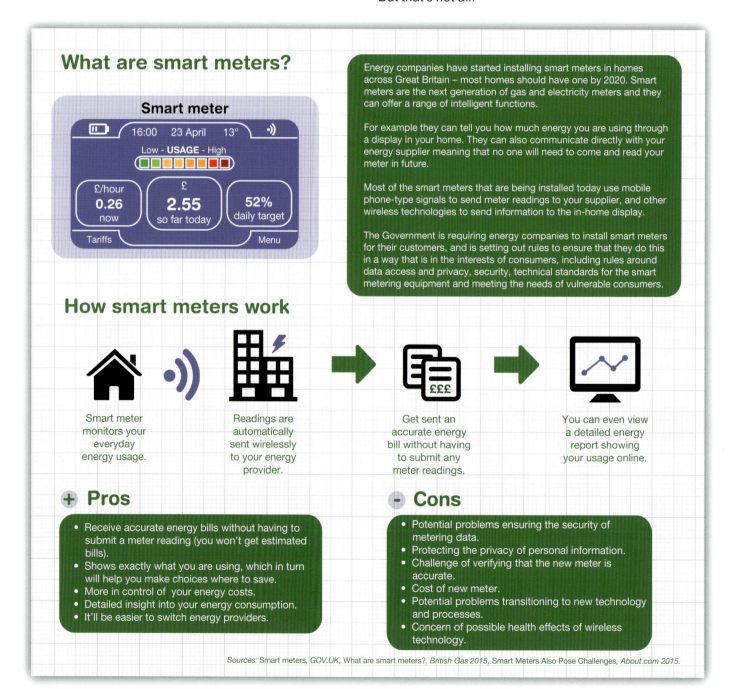

What are smart meters?

Smart meter

16:00   23 April   13°
Low - **USAGE** - High

£/hour
0.26
now

£
2.55
so far today

52%
daily target

Tariffs   Menu

Energy companies have started installing smart meters in homes across Great Britain – most homes should have one by 2020. Smart meters are the next generation of gas and electricity meters and they can offer a range of intelligent functions.

For example they can tell you how much energy you are using through a display in your home. They can also communicate directly with your energy supplier meaning that no one will need to come and read your meter in future.

Most of the smart meters that are being installed today use mobile phone-type signals to send meter readings to your supplier, and other wireless technologies to send information to the in-home display.

The Government is requiring energy companies to install smart meters for their customers, and is setting out rules to ensure that they do this in a way that is in the interests of consumers, including rules around data access and privacy, security, technical standards for the smart metering equipment and meeting the needs of vulnerable consumers.

How smart meters work

Smart meter monitors your everyday energy usage.

Readings are automatically sent wirelessly to your energy provider.

Get sent an accurate energy bill without having to submit any meter readings.

You can even view a detailed energy report showing your usage online.

+ Pros

- Receive accurate energy bills without having to submit a meter reading (you won't get estimated bills).
- Shows exactly what you are using, which in turn will help you make choices where to save.
- More in control of your energy costs.
- Detailed insight into your energy consumption.
- It'll be easier to switch energy providers.

- Cons

- Potential problems ensuring the security of metering data.
- Protecting the privacy of personal information.
- Challenge of verifying that the new meter is accurate.
- Cost of new meter.
- Potential problems transitioning to new technology and processes.
- Concern of possible health effects of wireless technology.

Sources: Smart meters, GOV.UK, What are smart meters?, British Gas 2015, Smart Meters Also Pose Challenges, About.com 2015.

The energy industry hopes that smart meters could be a step on the path to smart houses.

In the North East and Yorkshire a £54 million research project called the Customer-led Network Revolution (CLNR) is underway. Engineers and social scientists are working to find out how customers can reduce energy costs and carbon emissions in the years to come.

As part of the scheme they are working on ways to get smart meters to work with smart appliances to use electricity during off-peak hours, helping smooth demand on the grid because, in the words of the project:

'Users get a monthly smart energy report online or on paper, detailing where energy is used and where their money goes.'

'We make best use of power stations and the electricity network – and keep the costs down – by spreading our use of electricity over the day and night.'

Professor Harriet Bulkeley, is leading the CLNR social science research team at Durham University. Giving evidence to the House of Commons Energy and Climate Change Committee, she said her preliminary findings were that a sizeable minority of people liked 'gaming' a smart meter – trying to beat it and beat themselves.

In such trials, higher savings were typically found in homes with higher incomes and higher education levels, said psychologist Dr Gary Raw. But this new technology revolution is not just for affluent tech-savvy households.

For low-income households, energy use is absolutely paramount as it is one of the major expenditures.

Professor Bulkeley found that people had really appreciated being able to manage their household budgets with the help of smart meters, regardless of whether they had reduced their bills or not. The challenge, she told the committee, was to harness the energy knowledge that people do have – where to stand their clothes airer when the sun is shining – to information that can help them control their bills.

Power to the people?

As many an expert has pointed out, the cheapest energy is energy we don't use.

And that's why my neighbour is asking her supplier to send her an energy monitor straight away.

Some in the industry are even hoping that knowing how we use energy might make us feel less hostile to the companies that sell it to us. Stuart Rolland of British Gas puts it like this:

'At a time when energy companies are in the spotlight, and there's a lack of trust, smart metering is a great antidote to that, as it gives customers control.'

www.channel4.com/news

Consumers hostile to energy companies, suspicious of smart meters

By Harris MacLeod

More than eight in 10 (84%) UK consumers feel that energy suppliers maximise profits at the expense of customers and three-quarters (74%) believe that any savings facilitated by smart meters will be counterbalanced by increased prices to cover the cost of installation, according to a new report from YouGov.

'84% UK consumers feel that energy suppliers maximise profits at the expense of customers'

The Government plans to roll out smart meters, which improve household energy efficiency, nationally by the end of 2020. This is expected to be an enormous logistical and technical challenge for the energy industry, involving visits to around 30 million homes and small businesses to install over 50 million meters.

The YouGov report finds a high-level of antipathy towards energy suppliers, with 55% of consumers agreeing that 'energy companies treat people with contempt', as well as a fairly sceptical view of the purported benefits of smart meters.

'a quarter (25%) of consumers are concerned by the amount of data energy companies might be able to collect using smart meters'

Nearly a third (31%) of respondents say the aspect of smart meters that has most appeal is their potential to help cut energy bills, but 59% of bill payers surveyed say the cost of installation will lead to increased bills. Additionally, a quarter (25%) of consumers are concerned by the amount of data energy companies might be able to collect using smart meters.

Currently, only 7% of energy bill payers have a smart meter in their home.

31 July 2013

Big Six Energy Suppliers

The largest energy suppliers in Britain are referred to as the Big Six Energy Suppliers ('Big Six'): British Gas, EDF Energy, E.ON UK, npower, Scottish Power and SSE. They supply electricity and gas to both businesses and homes in Britain.

Cornwall Energy, an independent research group, suggests that Britain's 'Big Six' energy companies now have a 92.4% share of the market – the rest of the market is made up of independent energy providers.

Source: Cornwall Energy, www.cornwallenergy.com, 2015.

www.yougov.co.uk

Fracking threat to the UK

Fracking is a nightmare! Toxic and radioactive water contamination. Severe air pollution. Tens of thousands of wells, pipelines and compressor stations devastating our countryside and blighting communities. All while accelerating climate change. And to produce expensive gas that will soon run out. So why do they want to do it?

Extreme energy

Fracking is just a symptom of a much wider problem. As easier to extract energy resources are exhausted by the unsustainable energy consumption of the present system, we are resorting to ever more extreme methods of energy extraction. Over the last century the exploitation of fossil fuels has moved from tunnel mining for coal and drilling shallow oil wells to tearing apart whole mountains and drilling in a mile or more deep of ocean.

As existing energy resources are getting used up, the default response has just been to try harder; dig or drill deeper; go after lower quality resources or move on to more remote locations. This increasing effort has consequences: increasing pollution, more dangerous working conditions, greater greenhouse gas emissions, more land use and less resources available to other sectors of society.

At present we are on a course which leads towards a world dominated by energy extraction, one where most of the energy produced is used to run the extraction processes while people live and die in its toxic shadow. The present system's addiction to massive amounts of energy is driving this headlong rush towards oblivion and unless something is done to stop it we will all be dragged down into hell with it.

Tar Sands, Mountain Top Removal, Deep Water Drilling, Biofuels and Fracking are all symptoms of this scramble to suck the last and most difficult to reach drops out of our planet. Even more extreme extraction methods are being contemplated such as Oil Shale and Methane Hydrates, while existing methods are slowly growing more extreme as easier to extract resources are depleted.

Unconventional gas

The UK unconventional gas (and to a lesser extent oil) extraction is the main new threat, in the form of three different processes; Shale Gas, Coal Bed Methane (CBM) and Underground Coal Gasification (UCG). While there are a lot of differing technical details these processes all involve drilling large numbers of directional wells at regular intervals, coating the landscape.

The scale of these new more intense methods are like nothing we have seen before. Up until now the largest onshore gas field in the UK, Saltfleetby in Lincolnshire, had only eight wells. To produce the same amount of unconventional gas would require hundreds of wells to be drilled. To temporarily replace just one offshore North Sea gas field would require thousands of unconventional wells.

As well as requiring many more wells these methods also involve much more. Shale Gas and Oil require massive, slickwater hydraulic fracturing, to be carried out on every well. Millions of gallons of water, sand and chemicals are injected under massive pressure. CBM wells are also often fracked. UCG which involves setting fire to coal seams underground is even more extreme.

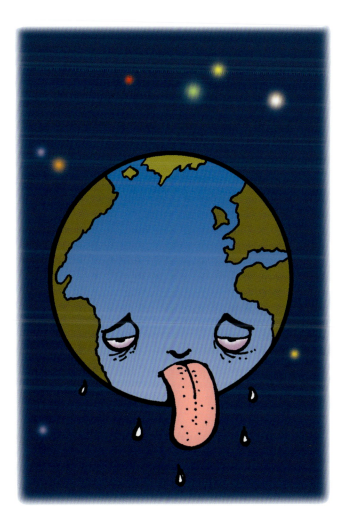

These unconventional wells also have much shorter lifespans, with production from a typical shale well declining by 70 to 80 per cent in the first year alone. This means that large numbers of new wells need to be constantly drilled to maintain production, even for short periods. In many areas of the US, unconventional gas is already peaking after less than a decade of exploitation.

Impacts of unconventional gas (and oil)

For all these processes water contamination is a major issue. All wells will eventually leak, as steel casings rust and cement rots, and unconventional gas (and oil) means many, many more wells. Contamination of groundwater has been a consistent feature of unconventional gas extraction, in the US, Canada and Australia.

The amount of water used in these processes and the amount of waste produced are also major issues. In Colorado, farmers are losing access to water as fracking companies buy up supplies. Meanwhile the vast streams of toxic and radioactive waste are a nightmare to dispose of, and attempts to get rid of this waste by injecting it into the ground are causing large numbers of earthquakes.

Air pollution is also an underappreciated threat from unconventional gas. In previously clean and unspoilt wilderness areas of the US, ozone levels now routinely exceed those in the centre of Los Angeles, while leaking toxic and carcinogenic hydrocarbon vapours are also common. Such pollution can be blown hundreds of miles from its source. Breathing difficulties are common complaints for those living in the shadow of these industries.

While targeted health studies of the effects of these developments have just not been done, what evidence there is shows major impacts. Cancer clusters, neurological and reproductive problems in humans and animals have all been reported and should be expected given the chemicals that are being emitted. In the area around the unconventional gas extraction, communities are getting sick and the response has been make people prove that the industry is the cause, or shut up.

Climate catastrophe

At a global level, there are already far more conventional fossil fuel reserves that we can afford to burn without causing catastrophic climate change. As with all unconventional fossil fuels unconventional gas (and oil) simply adds to this store of unburnable carbon. Widespread exploitation of unconventional fossil fuels could produce enough carbon dioxide to make the planet literally uninhabitable.

In the shorter term, methane emissions from these processes amplify the effects of the carbon dioxide emitted. Studies have shown that Shale Gas and CBM are worse than burning coal in the short term, and it is the short term that matters when considering potential tipping points in the climate system like melting arctic permafrost and the fate of the Amazon rainforest. UCG is even worse, with its direct carbon emission far higher than from the conventional exploitation of coal.

What can be done?

While all this may seem very bleak, there are rays of hope within this dark cloud. Unconventional fossil fuels are much more dispersed than conventional ones, meaning that in order to get them, many more communities are affected but must at least passively consent to their extraction. If these communities get organised to resist this invasion then it can be stopped. This is already happening is many places across the globe (for instance in Australia) but everyone needs to do their bit if this juggernaut is to be stopped.

Want to get organised? Want to take action? Get stuck in…: http://frack-off.org.uk/get-stuck-in/

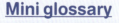

www.frack-off.org.uk

Mini glossary

Fracking – *a method to get gas or oil which uses highly pressurised liquid to force open cracks and fissures in the rock layer.*

Exploitation – *taking advantage of or using someone or something for selfish reasons.*

Extraction – *taking out, withdrawing.*

Heather could be UK energy source

Heather could help meet bioenergy target and cut greenhouse gas emissions.

Harvesting energy from heather could cut greenhouse gas emissions and help the UK meet its bioenergy targets, according to new research by experts at Durham and Manchester Universities.

Heather grows naturally throughout the UK's uplands, but land managers often burn it back to create better feeding grounds for grouse and livestock.

The study, published in the journal *Biomass and Bioenergy*, says this releases energy equivalent to burning 36,000 tonnes of coal every year.

If all the UK's heather was harvested as a bioenergy crop, it could produce as much energy as 1.7 million tonnes of coal a year, achieving 15 per cent of the UK's 2020 biomass target without taking any farmland out of production.

'We have a large source of very efficient, low-carbon energy growing naturally on our uplands, but we're releasing all its CO2 into the atmosphere without getting any energy from it,' says Professor Fred Worrall, from Durham University, who led the study.

'At the same time we're burning coal to satisfy demand, and that's a very dirty source of energy. Surely it would be possible to send the heather down the hill and stop burning the coal,' he adds.

The UK is committed to the EU policy of producing 20 per cent of its energy from renewables by 2020. A third of this is expected to come from biomass.

Elephant grass and short-rotation coppice are by far the most common bioenergy crops in the UK, but both require productive farmland which could otherwise be used to grow food.

By contrast, heather grows on largely unproductive heaths and moors. To assess its potential as a bioenergy crop, scientists burned samples in the lab and measured the energy released.

Using Countryside Survey estimates of heather coverage in the UK, they scaled their calculations up to the regional level, and subtracted the likely energy costs of harvesting and transporting the crop to incinerators.

As well as meeting a substantial part of the UK's bioenergy target, if it replaced its weight in coal, every hectare of heather could save 11 tonnes of carbon emissions a year.

But Worrall cautions that the industry could not take off everywhere. In parts of northwest Scotland, for example, heather grows too slowly, and the incinerators are too far away, to make it worthwhile.

Left to grow on its own, mature heather forms a blanket over the land. This makes poor grazing ground for sheep and grouse, and creates a large biological fuel store which can increase the threat of wildfire.

For these reasons, land managers throughout the UK routinely burn off patches of heather. But the practice has attracted controversy in recent years.

There are concerns that it could be degrading moorlands, causing peat to erode more quickly into surrounding streams. This can harm water quality and raise the costs of treating it for human consumption.

If heather were to be harvested for energy, it would first need to be cut and baled. The environmental effects of this are not yet clear.

Worrall believes the main barriers to using heather as a bioenergy crop in the UK are now cultural, rather than technical.

'From an engineering perspective it's entirely possible,' he says. 'I think we have shown that there would be real benefits too.'

'But there is a culture for burning among land managers, and my suspicion is that this would be difficult to overcome.'

29 June 2014

www.manchester.ac.uk

Mini glossary

Heather – *a purple-flowered plant that grows on moorland and heathland.*

US Navy's solar panels in space could power entire cities (or wars)

Solar panel satellites, built in space by robots that beam power down to Earth – sound like science-fiction?

Well, even the team behind the idea admit it sounds 'nuts' but that's not going to stop them trying.

US Navy scientists are developing the project which in theory could power entire cities – or military endeavours.

The solar panels will be made up of two types of 'sandwich' module to form a one-kilometre-wide satellite.

Each module consists of a photovoltaic panel on top to absorb the Sun's energy, an electronics system in the middle to convert it to a radio frequency and a bottom antenna layer to beam the power back to Earth.

Dr. Paul Jaffe, a spacecraft engineer at the U.S. Naval Research Laboratory (NRL), said: 'It's hard to tell if it's nuts until you've actually tried.

'People might not associate radio waves with carrying energy, because they think of them for communications, like radio, TV or cell phones.

'They don't think about them as carrying usable amounts of power.'

The implications of successfully developing the technology are profound. Obviously it could solve many of our energy needs in an efficient and green manner.

But it could also enable a giant lumbering war machine – like the US Navy – to conduct global operations without the constraint of transporting and refuelling traditional fuels.

When you consider the Pentagon is the world's largest consumer of energy (excluding countries) this will be of particular interest to US military planners.

The technology is promising and has even spawned new ways of testing materials for space conditions.

Jaffe said: 'One of our key, unprecedented contributions has been testing under space-like conditions.'

Using a specialised vacuum chamber at another facility would have been too expensive, so Jaffe built one himself.

He said: 'It's cobbled together from borrowed pieces.'

The vacuum chamber is just big enough for one module.

In it, Jaffe can expose the module to the simulated extreme cold of space and concentrated solar intensities (mimicked by turning on two powerful xenon lamps in the same spectrum as the sun).

By hooking the module up to a tangle of red and blue wires, he measures how well it radiates heat.

Jaffe says most solar panels orbiting with today's satellites are never tested in space-like conditions because the technology is already mature: 'But if you wanted to test anything under concentrated sunlight you would need something like the simulator we've put together here.'

Through trial and error, Jaffe has learned a lot. 'The capability we've built up with the testing and vacuum under Sun concentration is something that's pretty unusual.

'And we've actually gotten a couple inquiries from people who may want to use this.'

18 March 2014

www.huffingtonpost.co.uk

Mini glossary

Profound – *of great importance, very significant.*

Photovoltaic panel – *solar panels that converts energy from the sun into electricity.*

Wave and tidal energy: part of the UK's energy mix

An explanation of the energy-producing potential of wave and tidal stream energy in the UK.

Overview

Wave and tidal stream energy is electricity generated from the movement of wave and tidal flows.

Wave power is much more predictable than wind power – and it increases during the winter, when electricity demand is at its highest. Tidal stream energy is also predictable and consistent.

It is estimated the UK has around 50% of Europe's tidal energy resource, and a study in 2004 estimated the UK's technical resource at around 16 terawatts per hour per year (TWh/year) (4% of overall supply).

Wave and tidal stream potential

Wave and tidal stream energy has the potential to meet up to 20% of the UK's current electricity demand, representing a 30-to-50 gigawatt (GW) installed capacity.

Between 200 and 300 megawatts (MWs) of generation capacity may be able to be deployed by 2020, and at the higher end of the range, up to 27 GWs by 2050 (see the Renewable Energy Roadmap – https://www.gov.uk/government/collections/uk-renewable-energy-roadmap).

The UK is currently seen as a world leader and focal point for the development of wave and tidal stream technologies because it has an abundance of marine energy resource.

With its excellent marine resource and its expertise in oil and gas exploration, the UK is in a unique position to benefit from this type of renewable energy – and to develop related wave and tidal stream services. The industry is still in its early stages however, and further research is needed to determine how best to exploit these assets.

Tidal range potential

Studies have estimated the UK's total theoretical tidal range resource at between 25 and 30 GWs – enough to supply around 12% of current UK electricity demand.

The majority of this is in the Severn estuary (which has between 8 and 12 GW), with the estuaries and bays of the north west representing a similar amount and the east coast a further 5 to 6 GW.

The two-year cross-government Severn tidal power feasibility study could not see a strategic case for public investment in a Severn tidal scheme in the immediate term, though private sector groups are continuing to investigate the potential. Other potential projects assessed by developers at sites around the UK include the Mersey, the Solway Firth and the North Wales coast.

22 January 2013

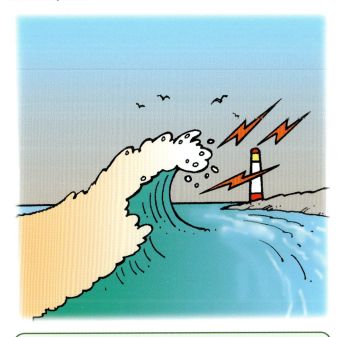

The above information has been reprinted with kind permission from the Department of Energy & Climate Change. © Crown copyright 2013

www.gov.uk

Mini glossary

Abundance – *plenty, lots of.*

Feasibility – *the measure of how possible something might be.*

Wind farm expansion will require fridges to be switched off at times of peak demand

Britain's increasing reliance on wind power in the 2020s could cause power shortages without a radical overhaul of the grid, including automatic control of household appliances.

By Emily Gosden

Household fridges and freezers will need to be automatically switched off at times when Britain's electricity demand is high, in order to keep the lights on as Britain becomes more reliant on wind energy, experts say.

The current electricity grid will struggle to cope with the number of wind farms expected to be built by the early 2020s because the power they produce is so intermittent, according to a report from the Royal Academy of Engineering.

A radical overhaul of the way the electricity system is managed – including a 'smart grid' that can control household appliances to reduce demand when power supply is inadequate – will be needed, it finds.

Britain will also need to build more power import and export cables to the continent to help manage variable wind power output, and develop storage technologies to keep surplus power for times when there is a shortfall.

The measures will be necessary to avert blackouts under a vast expansion of wind power – unless Britain instead builds an expensive new fleet of reliable power stations to be fired up as back-up when the wind doesn't blow, it found.

Professor Roger Kemp of Lancaster University, said: 'If there is a sudden peak in electricity demand the smart freezer would say, "Okay I'm going to switch off for half an hour until that peak is over".'

Consumers could negotiate cheaper energy tariffs for consenting to this and would not be affected by the temporary switch-off, he said.

'If you didn't have a smart grid and smart control of domestic equipment, you would probably find prices would have to go up more because the power-system people would have to build more power stations as back-up.'

The report says that 'the ability to manage demand to reflect the output from wind will be vital to the successful integration of larger amounts of wind capacity'.

However, it casts doubt on the viability of this solution, warning: 'There is much uncertainty on how effective it will be and at what cost.'

The report finds that the current grid can cope with 'up to a 20% contribution from wind power without the need for significant upgrades to the system and using existing balancing mechanisms'.

Beyond that threshold – expected to be crossed by the early 2020s – 'managing the system will become increasingly difficult', it warns.

The inherently variable nature of wind power will present problems when there is a mismatch between wind output and consumer demand – either too much wind or not enough.

'During periods of high demand, wind still often produces very low levels of output,' the report finds.

'At low levels of penetration [wind energy deployment], this should not be a major issue and, indeed, up to now security has not been compromised despite periods of virtually no output from wind and maximum demands. However, as levels of penetration increase, the situation can be expected to change adversely.'

If wind power continues to expand beyond 2020, days of negligible wind power could 'present problems for security of supply'.

In the reverse scenario, where wind output is high but demand is low, wind farm owners could increasingly have to be paid to switch their turbines off – an 'inefficient and costly' solution if it becomes more common.

10 April 2014

www.telegraph.co.uk

Mini glossary

Avert – *redirect, avoid.*

Negligible – *very little.*

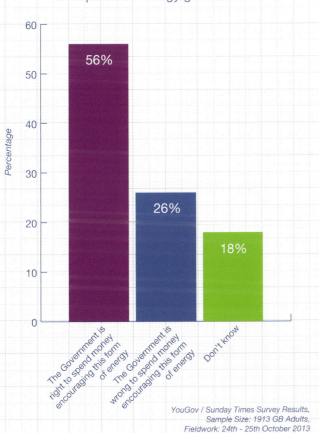

Do you think the Government is right or wrong to pay energy companies more to help develop wind powered energy generation?

- The Government is right to spend money encouraging this form of energy: 56%
- The Government is wrong to spend money encouraging this form of energy: 26%
- Don't know: 18%

Percentage

YouGov / Sunday Times Survey Results, Sample Size: 1913 GB Adults, Fieldwork: 24th - 25th October 2013

Beyond the 'poo bus': the many uses of human waste

An article from The Conversation.

THE C☉NVERSATION

By Sarah Jewitt, Associate Professor of Geography at University of Nottingham

A British 'poo bus' went into service [in November 2015], powered by bio-methane energy derived from human waste at a sewage plant.

For those of us who follow these matters – and my academic works include *Geographies of S**t: Spatial and temporal variations in attitudes towards human waste* – this was an exciting moment, a rare piece of good PR for human waste. After all, most societies strongly associate it with a sense of disgust. Poo threatens the health of around 2.5 billion people … and it smells bad.

Yet it also represents an important resource, used in lots of different ways throughout history. Though the 'poo bus' has captured the imagination there are many other uses for human waste.

Poo power

Although harvesting biogas from human waste is not a new concept (Assyrians were using it to warm their bath water back in the 10th century BC), the potential to simultaneously manage waste and generate power has attracted increasing attention in recent decades.

Modern waste treatment leaves behind sewage sludge that has traditionally been difficult to dispose of. However when the sludge is fed into a large vat, essentially like a stomach, and left to digest (an anaerobic digestion plant) it can produce valuable biogas and nutrient-rich digestate.

Biogas can be used directly as a fuel, cleaned up to create bio-methane or fed through a combined heat and power unit to generate electricity. The digestate

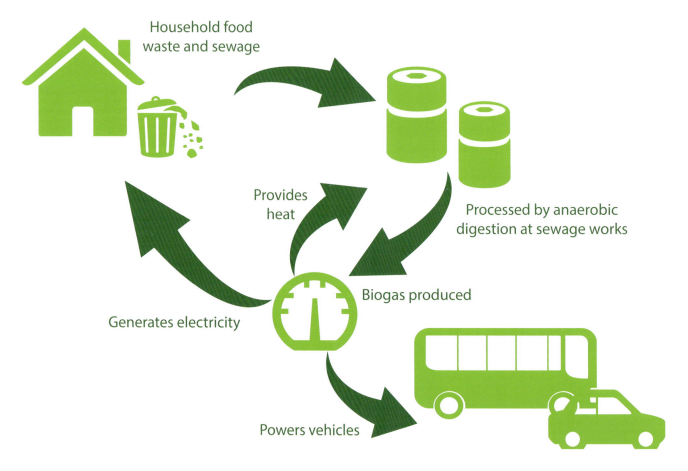

Household food waste and sewage

Processed by anaerobic digestion at sewage works

Provides heat

Biogas produced

Generates electricity

Powers vehicles

can be used as a fertiliser or soil conditioner, helping in the process to reduce methane emissions, enhance plant growth and sequester carbon through photosynthesis.

In rural China especially, low-tech biogas sanitation systems play an important role in killing pathogens while providing clean cooking fuel and fertiliser from the digestate.

Sweden and Germany are particularly big anaerobic digestion users. In Germany, sewage plants can sell their excess energy back to the national grid. Attractive tariffs designed to promote renewable energy have even meant many plants have started to 'feed' their anaerobic digestion units with purpose-grown energy.

Though the UK's biogas industry lags behind that of countries like Sweden and Germany, some sewage works are already releasing biogas into the national grid. With each adult producing around 30kg of dried sewage each year, there is lots of growth potential. If all of the UK's sewage plants adopted this technology, around 350,000 homes could be supplied with gas derived from human waste.

Toilet-fuelled transport

The environmental benefits of poo-powered travel are clear: bio-methane produces 95% less CO2 and 80%

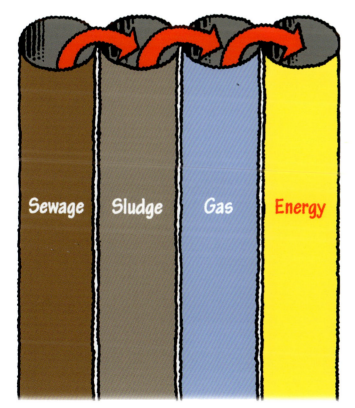

> The British 'Bio-Bus' that travelled between Bath and Bristol has 40 seats and can travel 186 miles on a full tank. It runs on human waste and leftover food.
> Buses that run on bio-methane produce approximately 30% less greenhouse gases than those that are powered by diesel.
> The first bio-methane fuelled bus in the UK was seen in September 2009.

less nitrous oxide than diesel as well as having no particulate emissions. In the UK, there is enough bio-methane to fuel half the country's large trucks.

Four years ago engineers developed a VW Beetle fuelled by bio-methane gas generated at the Avonmouth sewage plant near Bristol. This same sewage plant is now powering the 'poo bus' and it could do even more. Avonmouth produces around 17m cubic meters of bio-methane each year which, if exported to the grid, could meet the gas needs of 8,300 homes.

But Sweden, again, is a leader here. Their transport policy has prioritised the development of bio-methane for trucks and buses; an initiative that has helped to clean up the air and meet renewable energy targets.

At a smaller and more experimental scale, meanwhile, researchers at the Bristol Robotics Laboratory have succeeded in charging a mobile phone using electricity generated from urine. Using a microbial fuel stack, they have succeeded in taking advantage of the metabolism of live micro-organisms to create electricity from convert organic matter – in this case urine.

Other research teams working on similar 'pee conversion' technologies have succeeded in generating electricity, clean water and hydrogen from human waste.

If such technologies can be made to work on a bigger scale, the future for renewable power looks not only bright ... but yellow.

25 November 2014

www.theconversation.com

Energy crisis looms for UK, France and Italy

New Anglia Ruskin report shows threat to EU countries from natural resource shortages.

A new report launched 16 May 2014 warns that a number of countries in the European Union, including France, Italy and the United Kingdom, are facing critical shortages of natural resources.

Produced by the Global Sustainability Institute at Anglia Ruskin University, the natural resource maps indicate that some countries have less than a year of energy resources remaining and are almost entirely dependent on imports from the likes of Russia, Norway and Qatar.

By using the most recent data on known reserves and current consumption, the maps show that France has less than a year's worth of its own reserves of oil, gas and coal. Italy has less than a year of gas and coal, and only one year of oil. The UK fares only slightly better, with 5.2 years of oil, 4.5 years of coal and three years of gas remaining.

Some Eastern European members fare much better, with 73 years left of coal in Bulgaria and 34 years of coal in Poland. Meanwhile, Germany has over 250 years left of coal but less than a year of oil and only two years of gas.

By comparison, Russia has over 50 years of oil, over 100 years of gas and over 500 years of coal, based on their current levels of internal consumption.

Dr Aled Jones, Director of the Global Sustainability Institute at Anglia Ruskin, said:

'These maps show vulnerability in many parts of the EU and they paint a picture of heavily-indebted European economies coming under increasing threat from rising global energy prices.

'It is vital that those shaping Europe's future political agenda understand our existing economic fragility. The EU is becoming ever more reliant on our resource-rich neighbours such as Russia and Norway, and this trend will only continue unless decisive action is taken.'

Professor Victor Anderson of the Global Sustainability Institute added:

'Coal, oil and gas resources in Europe are running down and we need alternatives. The UK urgently needs to be part of a Europe-wide drive to expand renewable energy sources such as wave, wind, tidal and solar power.'

The full report, which also highlights issues such as food and water insecurity in North Africa and the Middle East, is available to download (http://www.anglia.ac.uk/ruskin/en/home/microsites/global_sustainability_institute/our_research/resource_management.html).

The maps are part of the Global Resource Observatory (GRO) project being carried out by the Global Sustainability Institute, which examines the relationship between the world economy and the environmental factors and resources it depends on. The GRO project has been generously supported by the Peter Dawe Charitable Trust.

The full GRO database of social, environmental and economic data will be made freely available to download this summer.

16 May 2014

European coal reserves

Years left (proved reserves divided by consumption)

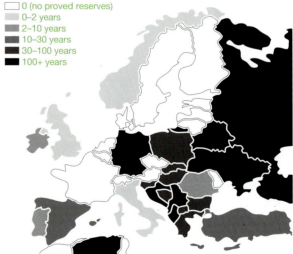

- ☐ 0 (no proved reserves)
- 0–2 years
- 2–10 years
- 10–30 years
- 30–100 years
- 100+ years

www.anglia.ac.uk

Activities

Brainstorm

1. What is a smart meter?

2. What is a biofuel?

3. What is an energy crisis?

Oral activities

4. As a class, discuss the following statement: 'Bioenergy and biofuels play a key role in the future of energy.'

5. Imagine a proposal has been put forward for a wind farm to be built in your local area. Role play a local council meeting, with one group of students acting as the councillors supporting the proposal and the other group of students acting as some local residents who oppose the proposal. Could the councillors be accused of not taking residents' concerns into account? Could the residents be accused of 'NIMBY'ism? What might be their concerns?

Research activity

6. Research possible sources of renewable energy that could be used instead of fossil fuels in the future. You can use the articles in this book as well as doing further research using the Internet. In your opinion, which is the most viable energy source? Write a short summary of your findings and conclusions based on the research you have carried out.

Written activity

7. Watch *Avatar* (12a) and write a review exploring how the director deals with the theme of energy.

Moral dilemma

8. As a class, discuss fracking. What is it? Why is it so controversial? Has it been utilised successfully anywhere? Or not so successfully? Read the article *Fracking threat to the UK* (page 17 and consider the author's point of view.

Design activity

9. Create a leaflet that will inform UK homes about the rollout of the smart meter programme. Include information about what a smart meter is and its potential advantages and disadvantages.

Key facts

➤ Coal has the most widely distributed reserves in the world and is mined in over 100 countries. (page 1)

➤ Oil and petroleum products supply a third of the primary energy used in the UK. (page 1)

➤ For an equivalent amount of heat, burning natural gas produces about 30% less carbon dioxide than burning petroleum and about 45% less than burning coal. (page 1)

➤ Nuclear is a clean form of energy in that it releases almost none of the CO2 emissions associated with fossil fuels. (page 1)

➤ A recent YouGov Reports publication has found that three in ten are spending 10% or more of their household income on gas and electricity. (page 6)

➤ According to figures from the Energy Saving Trust, the UK could collectively save nearly £4.4 billion on energy bills if householders took three energy saving actions in the home. (page 8)

➤ By avoiding standby, and making sure devices are not left plugged in or idle, a typical home could save between £50-£80 a year. (page 8)

➤ Whilst solar panels will work most effectively in bright sunlight, they nonetheless continue to collect energy from diffuse light even on a cloudy day. (page 9)

➤ [If emissions don't decrease], the World Health Organization expects 250,000 additional deaths to occur each year, caused by climate-related malnutrition, malaria, diarrhoea and heat stress around the globe. (page 10)

➤ By 2020, the government wants all homes and small businesses to have smart meters fitted. That means replacing over 53 million gas & electricity meters in 30 million properties. (page 13)

➤ British Gas says that 30 per cent of smart meter households spend an average of 18 minutes looking at their monthly energy reports – not once, but five times a year. (page 14)

➤ 84% UK consumers feel that energy suppliers maximise profits at the expense of customers. (page 16)

➤ A quarter (25%) of consumers are concerned by the amount of data energy companies might be able to collect using smart meters. (page 16)

➤ Britain's 'Big Six' energy companies now have approximately a 92.4% share of the market. (page 16)

➤ If all the UK's heather was harvested as a bioenergy crop, it could produce as much energy as 1.7 million tonnes of coal a year, achieving 15 per cent of the UK's 2020 biomass target without taking any farmland out of production. (page 19)

➤ Studies have estimated the UK's total theoretical tidal range resource at between 25 and 30 GWs – enough to supply around 12% of current UK electricity demand. (page 21)

➤ A British 'poo bus' went into service [in November 2015], powered by bio-methane energy derived from human waste at a sewage plant. (page 24)

Glossary

Biofuels and biomass – Plants use photosynthesis to store energy from the Sun in their leaves and stems. Living things, like these plant materials, are known as biomass. The wide range of fuels derived from biomass are known as biofuels. Corn ethanol, sugar ethanol and biodiesel are the primary biofuels markets.

Energy – A force which powers or drives something. It is usually generated by burning a fuel such as coal or oil, or by harnessing natural heat or movement (for example, by using a wind turbine).

Fossil fuels – Fossil fuels are stores of energy formed from the remains of plants and animals that were alive millions of years ago. Coal, oil and gas are examples of fossil fuels. They are also known as non-renewable sources of energy because they will eventually be used up: as they are finite, once they are gone we will be unable to produce more of them.

Greenhouse gases (GHG) – A greenhouse gas is a type of gas that can absorb and emit longwave radiation within the atmosphere. For example, carbon dioxide, methane and nitrous oxide. Human activity is increasing the level of greenhouse gases in the atmosphere, causing the warming of the Earth. This is known as the greenhouse effect.

Hydropower (or water power) – Energy which is generated using the movement of running water. This includes tidal/ wave power.

NIMBYism – NIMBY stands for 'Not In My Back Yard'. It refers to the attitudes of local residents who oppose developments such as nuclear power stations or wind farms in their area.

Nuclear power – A method of generating energy using controlled nuclear reactions. These are used to create steam, which then powers a generator. Nuclear power is controversial and subject to much debate, with supporters saying it is a greener and more sustainable alternative to fossil fuels, whereas opponents argue that nuclear waste is potentially hazardous to people and the environment.

Offshore wind farm – An offshore wind farm consists of a number of wind turbines, constructed in an area of water where wind speeds are high in order to maximise the amount of energy which can be generated from wind.

Renewable energy – Energy generated from natural resources such as wind, water or the Sun. Unlike fossil fuels, energy can be generated from these sources indefinitely as they will never run out.

Solar power – Energy generated by harnessing the energy of the Sun's rays.

Sustainability – Sustainability means living within the limits of the planet's resources to meet humanity's present-day needs without compromising those of future generations. Sustainable living should maintain a balanced and healthy environment.

Wind power – Energy which is generated using movement powered by wind. This is most commonly achieved via wind turbines, which are used to produce electricity.

THE MIDDLE STONE AGE
OF ZAMBIA,
SOUTH CENTRAL AFRICA